YOUR KNOWLEDGE HAS VALUE

- We will publish your bachelor's and
  master's thesis, essays and papers

- Your own eBook and book -
  sold worldwide in all relevant shops

- Earn money with each sale

Upload your text at www.GRIN.com
and publish for free

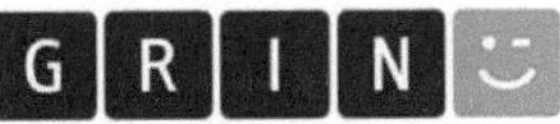

Bibliographic information published by the German National Library:

The German National Library lists this publication in the National Bibliography; detailed bibliographic data are available on the Internet at http://dnb.dnb.de .

Imprint:

Copyright © 2016 GRIN Verlag, Open Publishing GmbH
Print and binding: Books on Demand GmbH, Norderstedt Germany
ISBN: 9783668221239

This book at GRIN:

http://www.grin.com/en/e-book/322567/the-overlook-hotel-in-stanley-kubrick-s-the-shining

Angelo Rosato

The Overlook Hotel in Stanley Kubrick's "The Shining"

GRIN Publishing

Champlain College/St-Lambert

The Overlook Hotel

In Stanley Kubrick's *The Shining*

By: Angelo Rosato

Introduction to Research Methods

April 29, 2016

Contents

Introduction

In 1951 Stanley Kubrick released *Day of Flight*, his first feature film as director (LoBrutto 508). Although this film is largely unheard of, it is what started a career that some see as one of the best in film history. Twenty-nine years later, Kubrick released *The Shining*, a movie that completely changed how a horror film would be seen, shot and perceived from then on. *The Shining* is famous for its many subplots and details. Specifically, *The Shining* has at least two major subplots that on a first viewing would not normally be noticed. Only after thinking about the film, and watching it again would one realize that Kubrick had done something special. Stanley Kubrick's *The Shining* has one specific subplot that is a symbolic reference to how America was built from the ashes of Native Americans (Ager). The question asked when understanding this subplot would be, how does Kubrick depict said subplot through The Overlook Hotel, the setting and backdrop of this film? Through an argumentative and explanatory essay that has been approached with interpretive methods, a literary analysis will be provided on *The Shining*, proving that The Overlook Hotel is used by Kubrick as a focal point in dialogue, as a setting and as a character in order to depict that *The Shining* speaks specifically about how America rose from the ashes of Native Americans. The argumentative style is needed in order to convince the audience of the proposed thesis, and to convince the audience, the audience must first understand the film. The interpretive method, is used through the interpretation of Kubrick's film. The essay will first provide a context of the film and of Stanley Kubrick, followed suit by the arguments supporting the provided thesis, first analyzing The Overlook Hotel in dialogue, then as a setting and lastly as a character, an objection and counter-objection will then be provided before the essay is completed with a conclusion.

Perspective

Stanley Kubrick was born July 26, 1928 in the Bronx (LoBrutto 13). In his early life Kubrick did not care much for school and for that reason he attended his district school: William Howard Taft (15). After realizing that a district school did not suit his expectations for education – at the time he produced *Eyes Wide Shut* it was rumored Kubrick had an IQ of 200 (Acher) – he began skipping class in order to visit the local cinema; from that moment on he began to wonder, how he would be able to make better films than the ones he had been watching (LoBrutto 16). In his last year of high schol, Kubrick encountered a great proffesor, an art teacher then would inspire Kubrick to focus his life on art (31). Kubrick later attended City College, while being a proffesional photographer for *Look* magazine. His interest in litterature and art helped his progression in his self-education of film, and through this he became a director who is a "self-ordained film historian" (33). He would later go on to direct all-time classics like: *Spartacus* (1960), *Dr.Strangelove* (1964), *2001: A Space Odyssey* (1968), *A Clockwork Orange* (1971); and after *The Shining* (1980): *Full Metal Jacket* (1987) and *Eyes Wide Shut* (1999) (508-22).

In 1492, Christopher Colombus "sailed the great blue" and is considered the first to colonize the continent known today as North America. Right from the start conflicts between Natives and Caucassians were ignited: Europeans killed off ninety-five percent of Native Americans through war, disease and cultural genocide (Carrier). Years later, when the United States of America were pushing the frontier out west incounters with Natives happened often. To the point that sometime during the California Gold Rush, a policy was inacted. The Indian Removal Policy stated that Natives were simply obstacles in the goal to push the limits of the country. When Natives would try to fight back, US military forces would kill off tribes until others would move out, essentialy claiming land that did not belong to them. As the United States grew, Native numbers dropped (Carrier). This specific information will help the proposed thesis as it focuses on Kubrick's depiction of the hostile relationship between colonizers and Americans and the Native Americans. Moreover, to understand the thesis one must first understand the relationship that existed between Natives and their opressors.

The Shining is a movie adapted from Stephen King's novel of the same name. King, at first, did not necessairly enjoy the film as it offered many different aspects, such as specific details (i.e. Room 217 vs Room 237, Red Car vs Yellow Car – that the Torrance's drive, as well as the focus on Jack by King rather than the focus on the setting by Kubrick) in comparison to the book, including major plot points such as the death of Dick Halloran, the change in room number from 217 to 237 and minor details such as the car driven by the Torrance family (Ascher). The film is centered around Jack Torranc (Jack Nicholson) who is the newly-appointed winter caregiver at The Overlook Hotel, run by Stuart Ullman. Later, Jack drives his wife Wendy and son Danny to the hotel where they will stay for the winter, as he tends to the hotel and attempts to write a novel. During the tour of the hotel, the family meet Dick Halloran (Scatman Crothers), the head chef, who shares supernatural capabilities of telekensis with Danny. Jack quickly descends into maddness and darkness, being possesed by the hotel and eventually murdering Halloran. He later attempts to murder Wendy (Shelley Duval) and Danny (Danny Llyod) before being trapped in the outdoor labryinth of the hotel by his son, causing him to freeze to death. This critically-aclaimed film was directed, written and produced by Oscar winner Stanley Kubrick (*2001: A Space Odyssey*) and starred Oscar winner Jack Nicholson (*One Flew Over the Cuckoo's Nest*). It is the first film that sees Kubrick dabble into the genre of horror, and he does so in trend-setting style. Like Kubrick had done so many times before, he used his litterature and art genius to hide and tangle the simple story of *The Shining* with multiple subplots, most prominelty the one involving Native Americans (Dirks).

The Overlook Hotel: In Dialogue[1]

As mentioned, *The Shining* is written on an adapted screenplay, which was done jointly by Stanley Kubrick and Diane Johnson (a satirical novelist, this was her only film). In any film, TV show, theatre performance or even commercial, writing is the foundation for the production. In film it belongs to the four main aspects of film: acting, directing, writing and cinematography. Kubrick's screenplays were often written by Kubrick himself, giving the director more leeway to create the film he wanted, in his image, as stated by Mario Falsetto in the overview section of his book, *Stanley Kubrick: A Narrative and Stylistic Analysis*.

When analyzing how *The Shining* is a symbolic reference to the exploitation of Natives by Americans through The Overlook Hotel, one must examine the screenplay, more commonly known as the script. At the beginning of the second act of the film, named "Closing Day", the Torrance family is "en route" to the hotel, when Danny asks a question about something that occurred in the area where the hotel is situated (Kubrick 24. 9-14):

```
                    WENDY
        Hey, wasn't it around here that the
             Donner party got snowbound?

                     JACK
        I think that was farther west in
                  the Sierras.
```

---

[1] Note that all quotations from the screenplay of *The Shining* is provided by: http://www.imsdb.com/scripts/Shining,-The.html

> **DANNY**
> What was the Donner party?

> **24.**

> **JACK**
> There were a party of settlers in
> the covered wagon times. They got
> snowbound one winter in the
> mountains. They had to resort to
> cannabilism in order to stay alive.

> **DANNY**
> You mean they ate each other up?

> **JACK**
> They had to, in order to survive.

Although there are no references to Native Americans in this piece of dialogue, Kubrick is attempting to point something out to the audience. The Donner Party Tragedy is a real life, historical event that will forever be infamous to American Frontier history. In 1846, a group of ninety settlers traveled west, and on Christmas day were snowbound, in order to survive they turned to cannibalism before being rescued some time later (Limburg 28-9). Why it is relevant to the argument proposed is that Jack seems to be okay with the fact that people killed, and subsequently, ate each other to survive. It is a seed of greed being planted by someone who will be important to the hotel's well being throughout the winter. With this response, it seems as though Jack has already begun his descent into madness. His short relationship with The Overlook Hotel, which is subsequently symbolized as the United States, has already corrupted his humane mindset, turning him into a seeker of dominance (like the "country" he works for) rather than a compassionate father. Moreover, it is a way for the hotel to tell that greed is what is important; it is greed for land that caused the Americans to kill so many aboriginals.

Later in the same act, as Jack and Wendy are getting a tour of the hotel by Ullman, Wendy asks about the hotel's history and when it was built. Ullman, who is leading the tour, says something quite particular: "construction started in 1907, finished in 1909. The site is supposed to be located on an Indian burial ground, and I believe they actually had to repel a few Indian attacks as they were building it." (Kubrick 30.4). In general, when symbolically comparing *The Shining*, and more specifically The Overlook Hotel, to the treatment of Natives by Americans, the scene where Ullman provides a tour of the hotel to the Torrance's, contains the majority of the evidence that will eventually support the thesis. What is important to point out by this comment made by Ullman is that The Overlook Hotel itself is an obvious reference, by Kubrick, to the United States. It is a grand building that boasts its beauty through its extravagant artwork and powerful employees, such as Stuart Ullman. This is also shown earlier in the film, during the interview between Jack and Ullman. An American flag appears on Ullman's desk, symbolizing the pride of the country. There is also an eagle statuette in the frame, a symbol for freedom, something the Americans, as a country, value. Lastly, Ullman is wearing the colors of the American flag, symbolizing how the country becomes the person who works for it (Rice 121). Like the United States, the hotel is built from the ruins and ashes of the Native Americans.

Before this though, Ullman introduces Jack and Wendy to the main lobby of the hotel, The Colorado Lounge, where Wendy asks about all the Indian designs that are seen, like the carpets and paintings and if they are "authentic". Ullman replies, "Yes, I believe they are based mainly on Navajo and Apache motifs" (Kubrick 27.5). This is even more particular than the location of the hotel, as it exemplifies how Amerindian culture really had to be assimilated into the larger and more grand European culture during the times of colonization, as mentioned in the "perspective" section when Columbus was accused of "cultural genocide". The "cultural genocide", though, did not end with Columbus and early European explorers. Instead it continued with the aforementioned Indian Removal Policy, which forced Natives to blend in with the growing American society, or flee. This is what is truly represented by the décor in The Colorado Lounge, the forced and awkward Native assimilation that occurred due to American expansion. It is also important to note that Jack spend the majority of his time at the hotel in The Colorado Lounge. This represents the American presence in aboriginal affairs, even though assimilation had occurred.

Furthermore, through the dialogue that involves The Overlook Hotel, Kubrick points the audience in the direction of the subplot. The Overlook Hotel, through dialogue can be seen as a symbol for an America that was built, quite literally, from the ashes of Native Americans.

The Overlook Hotel, As a Setting

In order for any sort of story to be told, a setting must be involved. The setting for *The Shining* is The Overlook Hotel. The large and grand, secluded hotel on the outskirts of Colorado is the place where Jack Torrance loses his sanity and subsequently tries to murder his family. It is also the place where Native Americans were killed and where on top of those ruins, an American, profiting hotel was built (Kubrick 30.4). It must be mentioned, though, that when talking about setting in this essay, the focus will not be on the location of the area, as mentioned in the above argument. Rather a focus will be put on the subliminal backdrop that outlines the inside and outside of the hotel in order to further the thesis proposed, in that The

Overlook Hotel was Stanley Kubrick's key piece in referencing Native American mistreatment through *The Shining*.

The first thing that must be examined when analyzing the setting of The Overlook Hotel is the labyrinth. The labyrinth is a tourist attraction, as mentioned by Ullman, is 13 feet high, and is very hard to maneuver. Bill Blakemore, a contributor to documentary *Room 237*, says in an article about hidden meanings in the shining: "Kubrick carefully equates the Overlook Maze with the Overlook Hotel, and both with the American continent." North America was a continent unknown to man for the better part of human history, it is also big, and when finally discovered still had large parts to it be unknown. A comparison between North America, the physical continent can be made to the labyrinth. It is fairly unknown, hard to maneuver and is seen as a large piece of land that must be understood, visited and broken down. Once again, Kubrick places an importance on this because, Native Americans are widely considered to be the first Americans, living in North America thousands of years before any other peoples visited this vast, and untamed continent.

The second aspect of The Overlook Hotel is the décor. As mentioned in the above argument, the décor of the hotel was designed to complement Amerindian motifs. What is interesting about the paintings, carpets and overall design is that it is made subliminal to the audience. There is a specific painting of a chief that hangs under the stairs of The Colorado Lounge. It makes one wonder why Kubrick would do this, if he had been trying to inform us of the parallel between *The Shining*'s story and American/Native relations. Well the reason is this: there is no actual "Indian" met during the course of the film, instead Kubrick portrays a Native through another "visible minority", in Dick Halloran, who is promptly referred to as Chef (chief) Halloran. Again, it is subliminal – *The Shining* is a simple movie, it is a basic horror film, but the subliminal aspects is what give Kubrick and this masterpiece the ability to conduct such a powerful and meaningful subplot. The reason Kubrick enforces the subliminal aspect of the film is to represent how the average person always views the events that occur in their daily lives as what is presented to them, but never would the average person look past this to examine the subliminal and untold story of which their lives are based on.

The last setting aspect of The Overlook Hotel is the Calumet Cans seen in the stock room of the kitchen. The term calumet means peace pipe, an object used by Natives during peace treaties. In relation again with Halloran, in the scene when Dick shows Danny and Wendy the stock room in the kitchen, he has, behind him, many Calumet Cans, that have a chief logo on them, pointing the same direction as Dick's head is turned (Ascher).

Moreover, it is obvious through these three examples that the setting of The Overlook Hotel was used by Kubrick to demonstrate his subliminal subplot that focuses on the relation between Natives and Americans and how that relates to *The Shining*, and how this relation is fairly unexamined – and moreover, should be examined – by the average person.

The Overlook Hotel, In Character

In an attempt to prove how Kubrick uses The Overlook Hotel to further his powerful subplot, one must understand how The Overlook Hotel plays its part in the film as a character. *The Shining* is full of many interesting and complex characters, but the hotel itself will be the most important to the argument.

The elevator doors have become iconic in film history. The "river of blood" is something that will forever be remembered as one Kubrick's most famous shots, but why would something that is so simple, such as doors, become such an analyzed piece of art. The reason is that the doors have, like almost everything else in *The Shining*, is subliminal. The doors are often showed quickly, cutting back and forth from Danny's screaming face to the doors. Renowned film critic, Rob Ager suggests that the doors are a symbolic reference to a screaming face, specifically the screams of the Natives, and it is for that reason that the doors bleed; the bleeding allows the audience to make a connection of personification. The connection this makes to the primary argument is that Kubrick emphasizes, through the elevator doors, how implicated the Native Americans are in the foundation of the United States. There is even a further connection made to Danny. Danny, along with Wendy, comes off as the Native sympathizers. They represent the portion of the American population that acknowledges and realizes the crimes that have been committed against aboriginal people, and it is for this reason that Jack, the aforementioned employee of the United States (or Overlook Hotel) attempts to murder, both, Danny and Wendy.

Another way The Overlook Hotel is personified as a character is in its influence on Jack. A scene in which Jack is talking to Wendy about the hotel he mentions that it feels as if he had been in the hotel before (Kubrick 48.1):

JACK
```
I fell in love with it right away.
When I came up here from my
interview, it was as though I had
been here before. We...we all have
moments of deja vu, but this was
ridiculous. It was almost as
though I knew what was going to be
around every corner. Ooohhhhh...
```

This is an obvious reference to the twist ending that appears the end of the film, where Jack seems to have been at the hotel in 1921 as well as the present day. This is an important connection that is purposely place by Kubrick to confuse the audience deliberately. The meaning behind this connection has nothing to do with paranormal understanding, but rather it is there to have a deeper more meaningful message. The infamous final shot is done because Kubrick knows the audience will focus its attention in trying to understand the mystery. This is important because the true mystery of the film is the complex subplots that Kubrick presents and that must be understood, such as that of the relationship between Americans and Native Americans. Kubrick does this specifically for one reason: to tell the audience to "overlook" the major plot that has a minor difference in the world but rather notice the subplot that has a major implication in the world (Blakemore).

It is widely understood that Jack slowly becomes The Overlook Hotel as the film progresses. When the movie begins he is a schoolteacher that wants to write a new novel, but in the end he becomes a murderous father. It is believed that The Overlook Hotel possesses Jack, forcing him to become, quite literally, insane. This is important because this is Kubrick's way of informing the audience of how the people who are employed by The Overlook Hotel (or United States) have a tendency to reach an immoral extreme that causes them to change their character (Nelson 200). Mario Falsetto also points out: "the closer [Jack] gets to the Overlook, the closer his other (darker) personality comes to the surface" (Falsetto 166). When going through the days of the film (that is how the scenes are divided), one can easily recognize the deterioration in Jack's spirit. The Overlook Hotel is the inanimate object that controls Jack the way a colonizing or expanding government might have influenced settlers, forcing the humanity out of him or them (Nelson 200).

Furthermore, through the elevator doors, the influence on Jack and the photo at the end of the film, Kubrick manages to once again use The Overlook Hotel in all its capabilities to strengthen his subplot.

Alternatives

As there is no real objective to a plot of a movie, an alternative explanation can be offered. As this is a Stanley Kubrick film, there is obviously more than one subplot. A common subplot that can be explained is one very similar to the one concerning Native Americans, that being one of the Holocaust (Ascher). Why this could be pertinent is that Kubrick was raised with Jewish influences, as his ancestors were Jewish people who emigrated from Austria to the United States (LoBrutto 5-10). The reason that this theory, though, is not as popular is because there is not enough textual evidence in the film to suggest that it is a subplot as pertinent as that of the Native Americans, but when one analyzes this proposed subplot in more depth, there is a case to be made that the subplot actually exists. In 1976, four years before the release of *The Shining*, Kubrick proposed a period piece on The Holocaust, titled *Aryan Papers*. The project became a part of Kubrick's infamous "unrealized projects" list (which included: *Napoleon*, *The German Lieutenant* – another WWII screenplay, *Shadow on the Sun*, etc.) (Cocks). This is interesting to note because it confirms the love Kubrick had for German history, specifically World War II history. In addition, as seen before, Kubrick "rigorously transformed his interests and concerns into art" (Cocks 2). Interestingly enough, there is also an important shot that takes place in the film, suggesting a reference to WWII. As Jack thinks about what he wants to write, there is a still shot of a German typewriter, of the brand Adler.

Other alternatives also exist in Kubrick's masterpiece, such as hints of Kubrick staging the Apollo 11 moon landings. This alternative can slightly be examined by the shot of Danny rising after having a ball land at his feet. This alternative, however, is merely seen as a conspiracy, as there is no scientific evidence that supports this NASA mystery. Moreover, it is understood that multiple, unexamined subplots exist, all that is left to do is analyze these subplots, to further understand the greatness of this complex film.

Conclusion

To conclude, Stanley Kubrick's *The Shining* is a simple horror film that contains a subliminal, yet important subplot about the mistreatment of Native people by American settlers and European colonizers. Kubrick explains this subplot to the audience through the use of The Overlook Hotel. This theory is then further proven by how The Overlook Hotel is used in dialogue, as a setting and as a character. As mentioned countless times, *The Shining* is a complex film, filled with subplots and subliminal messages. Due to a lack of information, one cannot explore some really intriguing aspects to the film, like the obsession with the blue, red and white colors, Danny's Apollo 11 sweater, the references to animalistic society or even further explaining the Native American theory. Stanley Kubrick was able to do, with this film, what a very small amount of directors were able to do ever in their life time, and that is leave a lasting impact on the audience that makes them question the reasoning of the film itself. Kubrick is brilliant in his process of delivering his multiple messages, and will forever be unmatched in being so beautifully and intellectually mysterious.

Works Cited

Ager, Rob. "THE SHINING (1979) Analysis by Rob Ager." *THE SHINING (1979) Analysis by Rob Ager.* Collative Learning Systems, 2015. Web. 28 Apr. 2016.

Blakemore, Bill. "Hidden Meanings in The Shining?" *Hidden Meanings in The Shining?* Drummerman, 1987. Web. 28 Apr. 2016.

Carrier, Marc. *"The American People."* 330-201-LA. Champlain College, St-Lambert. 2016.

Cocks, Geoffrey. "Excerpts from The Wolf at the Door: Stanley Kubrick, History and the Holocaust." *Excerpts from The Wolf at the Door: Stanley Kubrick, History and the Holocaust.* Visual Memory, n.d. Web. 08 May 2016.

Cocks, Geoffrey. *The Wolf at the Door: Stanley Kubrick, History, & the Holocaust.* New York: P. Lang, 2004. Print.

Dirks, Tim. "The Shining Synopsis." *The Shining Synopsis.* Drummerman, 2002. Web. 28 Apr. 2016.

Falsetto, Mario. *Stanley Kubrick: A Narrative and Stylistic Analysis.* Westport, CT: Praeger, 2001. Print.

Kubrick, Stanley, and Diane Johnson. "The Shining." *Shining, The Script at IMSDb.* The Internet Movie Script Database (IMSDb), n.d. Web. 28 Apr. 2016.

Limburg, Peter R. *Deceived: The Story of the Donner Party.* Pacifica, CA: IPS, 1998. Print.

LoBrutto, Vincent. *Stanley Kubrick: A Biography.* New York: D.I. Fine, 1997. Print.

Nelson, Thomas Allen. *Kubrick: Inside a Film Artist's Maze.* Bloomington: Indiana U Pr., 1982. Print.

Rice, Julian. *Kubrick's Hope: Discovering Optimism from 2001 to Eyes Wide Shut.*
Lanham, MD: Scarecrow, 2008. Print.

Room 237. Dir. Rodney Ascher. Perf. Bill Blakemore and Jay Weidner. IFC Films,
2012. DVD.

Stanley Kubrick's The Shining. Dir. Stanley Kubrick. Warner Home Video, 1980.
DVD.

YOUR KNOWLEDGE HAS VALUE

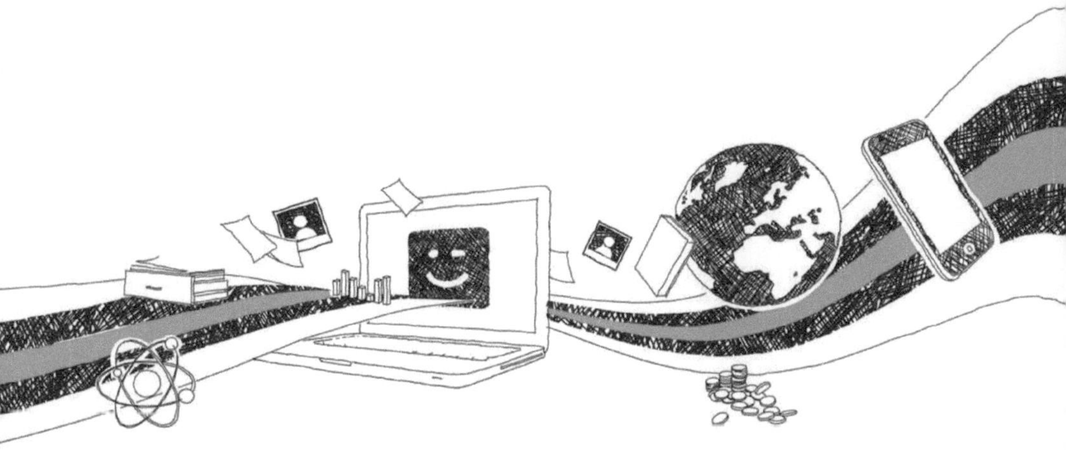

- We will publish your bachelor's and master's thesis, essays and papers

- Your own eBook and book - sold worldwide in all relevant shops

- Earn money with each sale

Upload your text at www.GRIN.com and publish for free

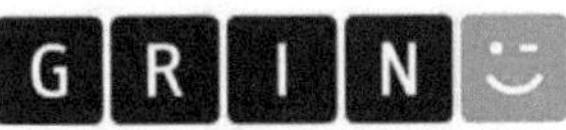